A Cashless Society

Nicolas Brasch

Rigby

www.Rigby.com
1-800-531-5015

Rigby Focus Forward

This Edition © 2009 Rigby, a Harcourt Education Imprint

Published in 2007 by Nelson Australia Pty Ltd ACN: 058 280 149
A Cengage Learning company

1 2 3 4 5 6 7 8 374 14 13 12 11 10 09 08 07
Printed and bound in China

A Cashless Society
ISBN-13   978-1-4190-3834-1
ISBN-10   1-4190-3834-6

Acknowledgments
The author and publisher would like to acknowledge permission to reproduce material from the following sources:
Photographs by AAP Image/Dave Hunt, p. 22; Alamy/Joe Wardman, p. 12/ Llene MacDonald, p. 14; Corbis/Christine Kolisch, p. 4/ James Leynse, pp. 18/ Polak Matt/ Corbis Sygma, p. 9; Gettyimages/ John Foxx, p. 19/ David Young-Wolff, p. 5/ Michael Matisse, p. 17; iStockphoto/ Richard Kano, back cover, p. 10/ Kay Ransom, p. 23/ Sami Suni, p. 11 bottom/ Sean Locke, p. 6; Newspix/Brett Costello, p. 7; PhotoEdit/Michael Newman, p. 8/ Photolibrary/Corbis Corporation, p. 15/ Steve Horrell, p. 16/ Workbook, Inc/Matsui Tim, cover, p. 13.

A Cashless Society

Nicolas Brasch

Contents

Chapter 1

A SHORT HISTORY OF MONEY

For thousands of years, people have traded
by swapping precious objects for goods.
People haved used many different objects
for these **transactions.**
People have used shells, feathers, and even tea bricks,
which are small bricks made by pressing
wet tea leaves together.

Tea bricks have been used
for money in parts of Asia.

Eventually most societies around the world created coins and bills to use as money.

Coins and bills were easier for people to carry around than the other objects they had used.

Today, thanks to technology and innovative thinking, there are many ways to carry out a financial transaction without the need to use coins and bills.

This has led to the term *cashless society*.

Chapter 2

CHECKS

A check is a piece of paper that **authorizes** the transfer of money from one person to another. Checks are issued by banks to their customers.

When customers want to use a check
to make a transaction,
they have to write four things onto the check:

the name of the person or company who is to receive the check

the date

the amount of money to be transferred

48 MARTIN PLACE

Pay *Smith County Soccer League*

The sum of *Three Million Dollars Only*

NOT NEGOTIABLE

Or Bearer

Date *June 7th 2006*

$ *3,000,000—*

BLACKCOURT LEAGUE INVESTMENTS PL ATF BLACKCOURT
LEAGUE INVESTMENTS UNIT TRUST

⑈00000⑈ 062⑈000⑈ 1178⑈0969⑈

his or her signature

A person who receives a check can bring it to the bank
and either exchange it for cash or
deposit it into his or her bank account.

Advantages of Checks

Checks make large amounts
of money transferable
without having to physically exchange
large amounts of cash.
This makes the transaction safer.

Disadvantages of Checks

The main disadvantage of using a check
is that a person could wrongfully pretend
to be another person and use his or her checks
to pay for things. This is called "**forgery**."
Thankfully most banks allow customers to check their
accounts by phone or computer at any time.
Access to account information helps to protect customers
from forged transactions.

Chapter 3

CARDS

During the twentieth century, different types of cards that carried out the functions of money came into existence.

The four main types of cards are:

- credit cards.
- debit cards.
- prepayment cards.
- smart cards.

Credit Cards

A credit card is a plastic card that people can use
to buy goods and services.
A credit card has a strip of magnetized material on it.
This strip holds information about the card holder.
When the card holder uses his or her card,
the information is transferred to the bank
or other institution that issued the credit card.

Unlike checks, which require the amount of money being transferred to be in the check holder's bank account, credit cards allow people to spend money that they haven't yet earned. They receive a monthly bill that outlines how much they have to pay back that month.

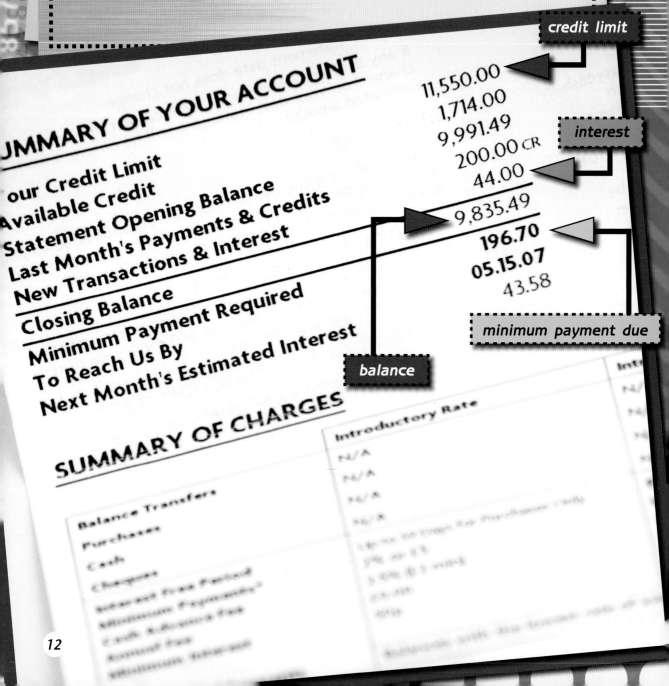

SUMMARY OF YOUR ACCOUNT

Your Credit Limit	11,550.00
Available Credit	1,714.00
Statement Opening Balance	9,991.49
Last Month's Payments & Credits	200.00 CR
New Transactions & Interest	44.00
Closing Balance	9,835.49
Minimum Payment Required	196.70
To Reach Us By	05.15.07
Next Month's Estimated Interest	43.58

credit limit

interest

balance

minimum payment due

SUMMARY OF CHARGES

Introductory Rate

Balance Transfers   N/A
Purchases   N/A
Cash   N/A
Cheques   N/A

Advantages of Credit Cards

Credit cards are easy to carry around.
They also allow people to buy goods and services
in an emergency if they don't have the money
to pay for them.

Disadvantages of Credit Cards

The main disadvantage of credit cards is that
people can get into financial trouble by spending
more money than they can afford to pay back.

Debit Cards

A debit card is a plastic card similar to a credit card. The major difference between debit cards and credit cards is that a debit card only allows a person to spend money that is in his or her bank account.

This helps overcome the main disadvantage of credit cards.

So people who use a debit card cannot get into
the same level of financial trouble
as someone using a credit card.
The bank issuing the debit card
won't allow a transaction to go through
if the card holder doesn't have enough money
in his or her bank account.

Prepayment Cards

Prepayment cards are usually made from plastic or cardboard.

They are cards that have a certain amount of money stored on them.

The money is stored as information in a magnetized strip or a microchip.

A person buys the card for the same amount of money that is stored on the card.

He or she then uses the card until the amount of money stored on the card has run out.

The most common use of prepayment cards
is for telecommunications.
People can insert their card into a public phone
and make telephone calls without the need
to put in cash.
Prepayment cards are very popular in Japan.

Smart Cards

Smart cards look similar to credit cards.
They are usually used for small transactions
and replace the complication of people always needing
to carry cash around with them.

Though smart cards are more popular in other countries, cities in the United States, such as Atlanta, Boston, and San Francisco, use smart cards instead of tickets to get on and off public transportation.
Riders swipe the card when they enter a rail station or bus, and the correct fare is taken from the card.
When the value stored on the card runs low, a person can transfer more money onto it.

Chapter 4

ELECTRONIC BANKING

Electronic banking involves the transfer of funds
through messages sent electronically
between two or more banks
or other types of financial institutions.
Two of the most common types of electronic banking
are direct deposits and automatic withdrawals.
Direct deposits are amounts of money paid into
a person's bank account from another account.
This is now a very common way for companies
to pay the wages of their workforce.

PiggyBank

Jenny Customer
54 Somewhere Ave
Cashtown, TX, 36672

a direct deposit

Super Saver Account Transaction Details

Date	Transaction	Debit	Credit	Balance
Apr 01	2007 OPENING BALANCE			$2,560.50
Apr 01	ATM	50.00		$2.510.50
Apr 04	FUNCORP		2,400.25	$4,910.75
Apr 05	CHECK 3422	110.00		
Apr 05	ATM	60.00		$4740.75
Apr 08	CHECK 3423	56.00		$4684.75
Apr 11	ATM	80.00		$4604.75

PiggyBank

Jenny Customer
54 Somewhere Ave
Cashtown, TX, 36672

automatic withdrawals

Super Saver Account Transaction Details

Date	Transaction	Debit	Credit	Balance
May 01	2007 OPENING BALANCE			$3,500.40
May 02	CHECK	60.00		$3,440.40
May 05	FUNCORP		2,400.25	$5,840.65
May 08	CHECK 3427	100.00		$5,740.65
May 11	SPARK ELECTRICITY	55.00		$5,685.65
May 12	ATM	60.00		$5,625.65
May 14	DIAL-UP TELECOM	39.00		$5,586.65

Automatic withdrawal involves the holder of a bank account
authorizing a company to transfer regular amounts
of money out of his or her bank account
and into the company's bank account.
People use automatic withdrawal to pay regular bills,
such as telephone or electricity bills.

Chapter 5

INTERNET BANKING

The creation of the Internet has changed people's lives in many ways.

One major change is in the way people manage their bank accounts.

Internet banking allows people to view their accounts, pay bills, and transfer money at home using their personal computers, all without having to go into a bank.

File   Edit   View   Favorites   Tools   Help

Back   Search   Favorites   History

Address

Home | Locate Us | Search | Customer Service | Privacy Policy

Online Services →

Personal | Business | Agribusiness | Community | About Us

Welcome

Internet Banking
Login options →
Register now →
Demonstration →

Online Services
Online Share Trading →
Apply Online →
Search for a property →
Home & Car insurance →

for your nominated not-for-profit organization*

*Terms & Conditions apply

Internet Banking
Register for National Internet Banking today for your chance to WIN.
Terms & conditions apply.

Click here

Tertiary Student or Graduate Package
Satisfy your appetite for life and you could win a new car and $2000.

Click here

News

Banks put major security procedures in place
to stop anyone but the real account holder
from accessing his or her bank account over the Internet.
This helps to ensure that people's bank accounts are safe.

Glossary

authorizes   gives permission to do something

forgery   illegal copying

transactions   exchanges or transfers of goods or money

Index